PRACTICAL TECHNOLOGY

WHAT IS A
DATABASE
AND HOW DO I USE IT?

Britannica
Educational Publishing

IN ASSOCIATION WITH

ROSEN
EDUCATIONAL SERVICES

Published in 2014 by Britannica Educational Publishing (a trademark of Encyclopædia Britannica, Inc.) in association with The Rosen Publishing Group, Inc.
29 East 21st Street, New York, NY 10010

Distributed exclusively by Rosen Publishing.
To see additional Britannica Educational Publishing titles, go to rosenpublishing.com

First Edition

Britannica Educational Publishing
J.E. Luebering: Director, Core Reference Group
Anthony L. Green: Editor, Compton's by Britannica

Rosen Publishing
Hope Lourie Killcoyne: Executive Editor
Nelson Sá: Art Director

Library of Congress Cataloging-in-Publication Data

Anniss, Matt.
 What is a database and how do I use it? / Matt Anniss. — First edition.
    pages cm. — (Practical technology)
 Audience: Grade 5 to 8.
 Includes bibliographical references and index.
 ISBN 978-1-62275-078-8 (library bound) — ISBN 978-1-62275-079-5 (paperback) — ISBN 978-1-62275-292-8 (6 pack)
 1. Databases—Juvenile literature. 2. Web databases—Juvenile literature. I. Title. II. Title: What is a data base and how do I use it?
 QA76.9.D32A56 2014
 005.74—dc23
                                                2013027173

Manufactured in the United States of America

Photo Credits
Cover: Shutterstock: Arek Malang. Inside: Dreamstime: 3dm1983 23b, Andresr 8, Cbpix 9, Delamofoto 41, Findog822 17, Godfer 25, Icefields 27, Instinia 39, Jcjgphotography 31, Jf123 11, Kurniawan1972 43, Miluxian 6, Mirobar 7, Monkeybusinessimages 15, 29, 35, 44, Morozena 37, Olesiabilkei 21, Tonnywu76 13, Wavebreakmediamicro 4, 23t, 33; Shutterstock: Arek Malang 1.

CONTENTS

Databases have many uses that help us run our daily lives, from chatting with friends on social media sites to looking up information for school projects.

INTRODUCTION

A database is a computer application that is used for storing, managing, and accessing information known as data. Information is entered into the database by an administrator or user, and organized into tables. Together, these tables and the information stored in them make up the database.

There are many different types of databases and they have many uses. Hospitals use them to keep track of treatments given to patients. Companies also use them to store information about their employees.

Databases can be simple or very complicated, with many tables storing all kinds of information. Some databases are so complex that database management systems are needed to administer them.

Databases can be of great use when researching school projects, for example, or investigating topics that interest you. They can be used to search for specific information about a person or subject, putting a lot of complicated information at your fingertips and in an easy-to-navigate format.

CHAPTER 1

DATABASE BASICS

Although computer databases may seem complicated, they exist solely to make life easier. Like a huge filing system, they store information so it can be accessed quickly and easily.

SIMPLE STORAGE

At its most basic, a database is a simple way of storing and presenting data in a convenient manner. The data can be anything, from text and numbers to images and video clips. When you log on to a social network, for example, you are accessing an enormous database filled with text, numbers, images, and video clips.

VIDEO DATABASE

Databases are everywhere and you may not have realized how often you use them. Did you know that the popular video-sharing website YouTube is a vast database of videos? It is possible to find videos by performing a "search" because details of every clip—its name, where it was filmed, who is featured in it, and who uploaded it—are saved on the site's database.

MAKE YOUR OWN DATABASE

One way to understand the principles behind databases is by making one about your friends, using paper or index cards.

- Decide what information to include about your friends, for example, their name, age, and e-mail address.
- Use a different sheet or card for each friend. Note down the data in the same order each time.
- Put all the sheets together in a folder or box. You now have your very own database!

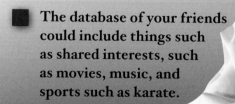
The database of your friends could include things such as shared interests, such as movies, music, and sports such as karate.

This librarian is helping a student find a book by searching a database listing all of the books that the library has on its shelves.

Database Searches

Not all databases are stored on computers. There are many everyday examples of "paper databases." You have probably searched one of these databases recently.

Database Book

One simple database you are likely to use all the time at school is a dictionary. A dictionary is a database of words and their meanings, with the words organized in alphabetical order.

Database Room

If you want to find out about a particular subject, you could go to the library. A library is a vast database of books. Libraries store books in a logical order to make it easier for people to find what they are looking for. In the past, you would need to browse different sections to narrow down your search. Today, most searches are carried out electronically.

LIBRARY SEARCH

If you go to a library to find a book on tropical fish, for example, you could ask the librarian where to find it. He or she could search the library's catalog of books, stored on a computer, for anything related to tropical fish. The librarian could then give you a list of books on tropical fish and show you where to find them.

If your library search for a book on tropical fish is fruitless, there are many other databases you could try, such as online encyclopedias.

COMPUTER DATABASES

Before computers, all databases were simply written down on paper, or in books, just like a dictionary. Paper databases are useful, but they have many drawbacks. Today, computers are used to overcome these difficulties.

PAPER PROBLEMS

Paper databases are often big and bulky. As they grow, you have to find more space to store all the entries. Paper records or book pages are also lost or damaged very easily.

PROBLEM SOLVING

Computer databases are quick, reliable, and much smaller than paper databases. If you need more storage space, you can buy another hard drive (the part of a computer that stores data) and add it to the database system. You can also back up your files onto another hard drive.

A VARIETY OF USES

A lot of organizations use computer databases. At many hospitals, for example, doctors use databases to access, read, and update their patients' medical records. The police also use databases to keep records of criminals.

THE DATA BIO

In the 1960s, a scientist named Charles Bachman created the first computer database. His system, called Integrated Data Store (IDS) was the first to allow people to store, organize, and manage information on a computer. In 1973, Bachman was awarded the A.M. Turing Award by the Association of Computer Machinery in honor of his pioneering work.

Charles Bachman's original database was simple. Modern databases can be used to store anything. For example, the police store fingerprints of criminals on databases.

Internet Databases

The Internet has changed the way people access information. It has also changed the way they interact with databases. Some of the most common activities on the Internet involve database searches.

Hidden Databases

Many different websites use databases to store and organize information. Online shopping websites, such as www.amazon.com, use a number of databases to make their site easy to use. For example, there may be a database storing shoppers' personal details, another featuring details of products for sale, and another keeping track of stock levels (how many copies of each product they have in their warehouse).

Massive Databases

Some databases used by Internet companies and websites are immense. For example, the Google web search facility, that allows you to search the World Wide Web for specific pages, is based on an immense database featuring details of billions of websites. In fact, it is so big that it has to be stored on hundreds of thousands of storage computers, called servers.

ONLINE DATABASES

Online databases are websites designed to help people find information quickly and easily. Popular examples include The Internet Movie Database (www.imdb.com), which contains information on everything to do with movies, and Baseball Reference (www.baseball-reference.com), which holds more than 100 years of player, game, and team records.

The Internet Movie Database is an online database dedicated to movies. Rotten Tomatoes (www.rottentomatoes.com), is based around a searchable database of movie reviews.

CHAPTER 2

DATABASE PARTS

Data is the most important part of any database, and the reason for its existence. There are many different types of data—from letters and numbers, to pictures and videos.

EVERYTHING IS DATA

Data can be any piece of information. On its own, that information may not be particularly significant, but gathered together with other information in a database, it has more meaning.

DATA IS EVERYWHERE

The information in a database can be about anything. Take an address book, for example. Each of the names, telephone numbers, and addresses is a piece of data. Another example is an MP3 player, which uses a database to keep track of all the songs stored on it.

DATA IS HELPFUL

Data can be information on specific subjects, such as social studies, history, math, or health. In fact, there are many databases available that can be used for researching school projects, or to answer personal questions.

■ The songs on an MP3 player are all individual pieces of data, while the player itself holds a big database.

FINDING USEFUL DATABASES

Many school and public libraries have databases to help with schoolwork. To find out what databases are available, just ask. Some school districts also list available databases on their websites. Here is an example from the public school board in Gwinnett County, Georgia: www.gwinnett.k12.ga.us/media-resources.nsf/pages/ElementaryAll~Elementary

Data, Information, and Knowledge

Pieces of data on their own can often be of little use. However, databases put information into a new or different context so that the data makes sense. They give data a new structure so that the information becomes more useful and accessible to us.

The Importance of Structure

To show the importance of structure, here is a simple example. Each of the words in the sentence "I have a dog" is a piece of data. On their own, these words mean something, but have more meaning and specificity when used together. The words need to be part of a structure in order for them to make sense. In this example, the structure is the sentence. This structure turns the data into information that we can all understand.

Knowledge Is Power

Databases make information more useful to us. They can turn seemingly random data into a practical resource. Once data is turned into useful information, we gain knowledge that we can use to make decisions.

HOW DATABASES HELP

Every week, sports coaches make decisions about which players to pick for certain matches. Baseball coaches may do this with the help of a database, listing the name of every player, the balls he has hit, the catches he has made, and the number of home runs he has scored. By using a database to consider all these factors, coaches can pick what they think is their best team.

Sports coaches keep records of player statistics on databases in order to help them plan team tactics and coaching sessions.

Fields, Records, and Tables

To be of use, a database must store information in a certain way, using a logical set of rules. Once this has been done, the data can be easily accessed and examined.

Field Fun

Most databases are structured into tables, featuring rows and columns that make up a grid. Each of the squares or rectangles within the grid is known as a "field." Data is stored in these "fields." Each column in the database contains a specific type of data, known as the "field type."

Important Records

If you read each row from left to right, you will see a complete record of the data stored about each field type. As a result of this, each row is known as a "record." The records of the database together make up what experts call a "dataset."

Every database must have a "key field" that is unique to each record. For example, in databases of people's personal details, this is usually a person's name.

DATABASE IN DETAIL

The best way to understand the structure of a database is to examine one. Here is a class record put together by a teacher.

Key Field
The key field is the information that is always unique to that record, in this case the pupil's name.

Record
Records contain data usually about the same person, company, or topic.

	CLASS	D.O.B.	ADDRESS	E-MAIL
ews	6A	09/22/2001	114 Oak Street	milly@mail.net
r	6A	10/14/2001	232A Willow Lane	brian@ deanemail.com
an	6A	01/30/2002	APT4C Beech Tower	Hoff9janey@ email.com
ds	6A	06/22/2002	764 Ash Avenue	woodsy@ ashhaus76.org

Field Type
In this database table, there are five field types. This field type is "date of birth."

Field
The boxes that make up the database table are known as "fields."

Dataset
The four pupil records in this example make up the dataset.

FIELD ATTRIBUTES

Databases can be as simple or as complicated as needed. They can also be tailored to fit the user's needs through the use of "field attributes." Tailoring a database can make it more efficient for its user.

FIELD RESTRICTIONS

Database creators use field types to restrict, or specify, the type of data that can be stored in each field type. This could mean allowing only numbers, letters of the alphabet, or even a specific number of letters within that field.

PRACTICAL RESTRICTIONS

Using the school database example on page 19, the field attribute for the "name" field would be letters only. The "date of birth" field would also be restricted to numbers and the "/" character.

REQUIRED ATTRIBUTES

Field attributes can also be used to specify whether a field must be filled in (making it "essential" or "required") or can be left blank ("optional"). It is even possible to set up a field to automatically add together the numbers contained within some of the other fields in the database.

FORMS AND DATABASES

Many websites, including social networks, use sign-up forms for new users to add their details to a membership database. Many of these forms specify that certain details, such as name, age, and an e-mail address are "required." This is because the field attributes of the membership database state that they are essential.

Social networks will not let you join unless you fill in key personal details, such as your name and date of birth. These are the database's "required fields."

CHAPTER 3

DIFFERENT DATABASES

Different databases are used for different jobs. As a result of this, some databases can be classified by what they are used for. Some databases are tightly controlled, while others can be updated regularly.

DIFFERENT FUNCTIONS

Analytical databases are used to keep track of numbers and statistics. They cannot be updated once they have been created, and are used mainly for research. Companies use them to keep track of the number of products they have sold, or money that has been paid to them. A bank statement, showing monthly income, outgoings, and the funds in an account, is an example of a basic analytical database.

DATA UPDATE

Analytical databases are "read-only" databases. This means that you can look at the data but you cannot change it. Databases that allow users to change or update the data are known as "operational databases." Websites such as Facebook are operational databases.

Social networks are websites built around operational databases, which allow you to update your record whenever you like.

UPDATING YOUR PROFILE

When you update your profile on a social network such as Myspace or Facebook, you are updating the website's database. Your profile is a single record on the database. When you update your likes, dislikes, and profile picture, you are updating different fields in Facebook's database.

Database Models

Large databases often contain huge amounts of data, so a lot of thought must be put into how they are structured. There are many different ways of structuring databases—known as "database models."

Understanding Models

A database model is the way a database is set up, and therefore how the data within it is stored, organized, and changed.

A good comparison is a school. If you think of the school building as the database and the students as the data, the database model would be the way of arranging the students into different classes inside the building.

THE FLAT-FILE MODEL

The most basic database model is the flat-file database. This is a simple table, similar to the example on page 19. You could quite easily make a similar database about your family on a sheet of paper, with fields for height, age, eye color, and favorite music.

You can make databases about anything, from the color of your friends' hair and eyes to their personal details. The type of database you need to use will depend on how you organize the information.

Hierarchical Databases

Most of today's complex databases are not one simple table, but rather many small databases that are linked together. There are many ways to link databases. In the past, one of the most commonly used methods was by a "hierarchical database" model.

Database Tree

A hierarchical database links many smaller databases together like a family. There is a "parent" database and many "children," or lesser databases. Each of these "children" can also have children themselves. Unlike real families, however, each "child" in a database can have only one parent.

Business Use

Hierarchical databases are useful for companies that need to keep track of a lot of customer information. They are used by online stores such as Amazon.com. The model allows them to create individual databases for each of their many customers (the "children" mentioned above), linked to a "parent" database (their master list of customers).

DATABASE HIERARCHY

An example of a hierarchical database can be seen in the way medical records are stored by hospitals. Each box in the diagram represents a database table. These tables are linked together in a hierarchical structure, with the doctor's list of patients at the very top, and smaller tables featuring details of patients' medications and known problems at the bottom.

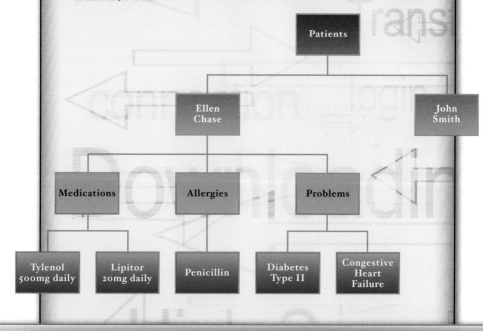

The way this hierarchical database is structured is similar to a family tree, which would feature grandparents at the top, parents below, and children at the bottom.

Relational Databases

Today, very few people use hierarchical databases because they make finding information difficult. Instead, most people use "relational databases" that give them access to information at the push of a button.

It's All Relational

Relational databases are much easier to use, because you can search for specific data, or group data together to compare it. This is possible because all of the records, and the data within them, are linked.

A good example of a relational database is the address book on a smartphone. You can browse through it to find someone's telephone number, search by their name, or ask it to display names and e-mail addresses.

Smart Search

Here's another example. If you wanted to buy a new smartphone, you might want to check out all the models available on a cell phone store's website. Using the site's database, you could compare phones by price, features (camera, MP3 player, and so on), or manufacturer (Apple, Samsung, and so on).

THE DATA BIO

British-born American computer scientist Edgar F. Codd was born in 1923. In 1970, while working for computer company IBM in San Jose, California, he created the first relational database. Codd continued to work for IBM until the 1990s.

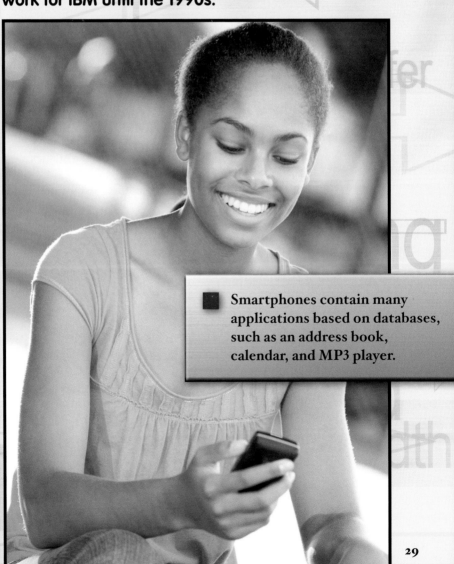

Smartphones contain many applications based on databases, such as an address book, calendar, and MP3 player.

Client-Server Databases

Many of the databases we access are on the Internet. These are known as client-server databases. They allow you to use your computer to access a wide range of information.

Familiar System

Client-server databases take their name from the relationship between the computer accessing the database (known as the "client"), and the computer storing it (known as the server). Client-server databases can be accessed 24 hours a day, over the Internet. Users gain access to the database using an interface on their own computer, such as the browser software used to view web pages.

Search Engines

Internet search engines, such as Google, are a great example of client-server databases. When you search for web pages, pictures, videos, or music tracks using Google Search, your computer (the client) sends a request for information to Google's database (the server). The server then processes the request, and displays the results.

CLIENT-SERVER SHOPPING

The iTunes Store, where you can buy and download music MP3s, runs on a client-server database system. The interface used for accessing the database is the iTunes software on your computer or smartphone. The server is Apple's huge database of songs for sale.
If you decide to buy a song, the database will process your request, and then transfer the MP3 to your computer or smartphone.

By 2013, 50 billion apps had been downloaded from iTunes' database.

CHAPTER 4

HOW DATABASES WORK

To read, search, browse, or change a database, you must connect to it. How you do this will depend on whether the data is stored on your computer, or elsewhere, such as on the Internet.

COMMAND SHELL

To connect to the database you can use a "command shell." This is an interface on your computer, such as a database software program. Most computer operating systems, such as Windows or Apple OS, are also an interface. The part you interact with every day is a command shell for the database running on your computer.

NETWORK SOCKET

Another way of connecting to a database is through a network socket. This is used when connecting to a database over any computer network, such as the Internet. With this method, your computer must communicate with another to gain access to the database.

NETWORK EXPLANATION

Here is how a network socket database connection works, using the example of your family doctor accessing medical records.

- The doctor opens the program she uses to access patients' medical records, which are stored on another computer in the hospital.
- Before connecting to the database, she confirms her identity by typing in her name and security code. She then requests your medical records.
- Her computer sends a request for your records across the network, to the computer storing the database.
- The database computer processes her request, and sends back your medical records.

Doctors can gain access to the database storing your medical records using a network socket connection.

Database Speak

The databases we use in our daily lives are often very simple to use. However, the computer languages that make them work efficiently can be hugely complicated.

Language Lesson

A computer language is a series of simple instructions, called commands, used to tell a computer, or a software program such as a database, how to perform certain tasks.

Structured Query Language

There are many different computer languages used by databases, but there is one that is more popular than the others. It is called SQL, which is short for Structured Query Language.

SQL Basics

SQL was designed to allow database users to search for and make changes to data across many different databases. These tasks are performed using a series of simple commands. If you learn these commands, you should be able to find the data that you are looking for quite easily.

SQL EXPLAINED

Imagine you had just met someone called Melissa and wanted to search for her profile on a social network such as Facebook. You would type "Melissa" into the search box at the top of the web page. The social network would then turn it into the following SQL command, in order to search its database:

SELECT * FROM people WHERE firstname = "Melissa"

Now let us break down the command:

SELECT * FROM people
This tells the database to look in the table called "people."

WHERE firstname
This narrows down the search to a specific field within the table, namely first name.

= "Melissa"
This tells the database you are looking for the word "Melissa."

If you have just met someone and want to search for him or her on social networks, SQL commands can help you.

CHAPTER 5

DATA SECURITY

Databases hold all sorts of information about our lives, from medical and health care records and personal information to bank account details and school grades. It is vital to keep them secure and safe.

SAFETY CONCERNS

A lot of the information stored on databases is sensitive or highly personal, so keeping it safe is one of the biggest tasks facing many companies and organizations. How would you feel if your medical records fell into the wrong hands, or if someone gained access to your Facebook account and started posting unpleasant things about your friends? Someone could even set up a profile using your details.

SECURITY THREATS

There are many threats to database security. These include computer failure such as when a computer "crashes," accidental damage, and deliberate attacks from criminals known as hackers. Hackers are cybercriminals who look for weaknesses in computer systems in order to steal personal information, or cause damage to the system.

facebook

Facebook Safety

facebook
Safety

Social networks take data security very
seriously because they hold so much
personal data on users in their databases.

WHEN HACKERS ATTACK

If hackers find a weakness in a database, the
results can be awful. In April 2011, electronics
giant Sony had to shut down the PlayStation
Network, its online gaming system. Hackers
had stolen the personal details, including home
addresses, of about 77 million players. It took
Sony 24 days to fix the database and make
the Playstation Network secure once more.

Securing Data

Losing friends' contact numbers, important school projects, your MP3 collection, or treasured photos, can be upsetting. That is why it is so important to keep your data safe.

Smart Start

A good place to start is by protecting the data on your computer or smartphone. One way to do this is to make a back-up, or a copy, of the data. Many companies allow you to back-up your files to computers over the Internet.

Password Protection

You can also keep data safe by using password protection. A password is a secret code, word, or phrase that only you know. If your data is protected, nobody else can gain access to it.

STAYING SECURE ONLINE

When you sign up to join a social network, you have to select a unique user name and password. Every time you use the site, you will be asked to enter these secret details. If you join a number of networks, use a different password for each one to ensure you keep your data safe.

Apple offers its computer, smartphone, and tablet users back-up storage on its "iCloud" service, which allows users to save copies of their MP3s, apps, and other documents online.

39

CHAPTER 6

THE FUTURE OF DATABASES

Today, computer database systems are so advanced that every little detail of our lives can be noted down and stored online, even if we do not realize it.

So Much Information

Take a moment to think how much data about your life is stored on databases. To begin with, the government holds records of where and when you were born, and where you now live. Your school has a record of your grades, and what projects you have completed. Your doctor or local hospital keeps your medical records, while your dentist has your dental records, too.

Data Trail

In addition to all these records, there is also any information *you* may put online—such as the likes and dislikes you list on social networks, the photos of your last summer vacation, and the e-mails you send using services such as Gmail, Yahoo!, or Hotmail. Every time you search the web, your search query is automatically stored on a database.

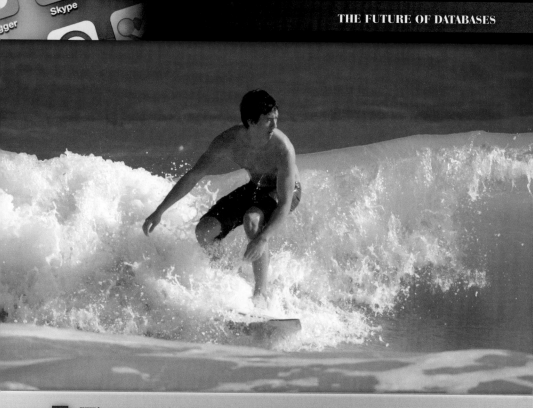

When you upload your vacation pictures to websites such as Facebook, Flickr, and Instagram, they are stored in giant databases.

DATA BANK

Many Internet companies already use your personal data to make money. The advertisements you see when you log on to Facebook are specifically targeted at you based on data you put online. For example, if you list "cats" and "rap" in your "likes," you will see advertisements for cat food and rap music.

Database Living

We know that almost every tiny detail of our lives is now stored in databases, and the volume of data will only increase in the future. So how will that data be used in the years ahead?

Positive Impact

As databases can be used to keep records of everything, experts think they could be utilized to help organize and run our lives more efficiently. For example, a database could be used to automatically re-order food when the refrigerator becomes empty. A database could automatically pay for tickets when we get on a bus or train, and databases could download useful information for forthcoming school projects and homework assignments.

Keeping Our Personal Details Safe

Some people think there is too much of our personal data online. These people say we cannot be sure that our personal data is not being used by companies and government agencies to spy on us. They think this is dangerous, but the government says the data can be used to keep us safe from terrorist attacks, or to govern the country.

DATA CONTROVERSY

In June 2013, former U.S. government employee Edward Snowden told journalists that the National Security Agency has the technology to spy on the databases of major Internet companies, such as Google and Apple. This caused controversy, because the information held by these companies is supposed to be private. President Obama denied the claims, but was forced to admit that the U.S. government does monitor Internet data as part of its plan to tackle terrorism.

The U.S. government says that monitoring our personal data could help keep the country safe from terrorism.

DIVE INTO DATABASES

Databases may seem daunting at first but as we have discovered, they can be very easy to use. They can also be enormously helpful in our daily lives. Why not dive straight in and find out what databases can do for you?

You can use databases to organize your life and to share the things you love with family and friends around the world.

TOP TIPS FOR USING DATABASES

1. Search an online encyclopedia to find out about almost anything. With an account, users can access www.britannica.com where paid-for content by Britannica is available. The site provides useful information for school projects or general hobbies and interests.

2. Browse the shops at www.amazon.com. Online shopping sites are built around giant databases, listing all of the products for sale.

3. Find out more about the world we live in, by checking out the CIA World Factbook at: www.cia.gov/library/publications/the-world-factbook/index.html.

4. Store all your friends' phone numbers and e-mail addresses in an address book on your smartphone or computer.

5. Search Google's database of websites and web pages at www.google.com.

6. Update your likes and dislikes on a social network such as www.facebook.com.

7. Upload a clip to www.youtube.com, and contribute to the world's largest online database of videos.

administer To manage something.

analytical databases Databases used to keep track of numbers or statistics.

browse To look through something.

commands Instructions to a computer or software program, such as a database, to perform a specific task.

computer languages Systems of simple commands that instruct computers to perform tasks.

database models Ways of structuring a database.

fields Data storage spaces in databases.

field type The name of a column in a database table, explaining the type of data featured (such as first name, last name, or age).

hackers Criminals who specialize in targeting computer systems, usually with the purpose of causing damage or stealing data.

hierarchical databases Databases structured like a family tree, with a "parent" database at the top, and "child" databases below.

income Any money received by an individual or company.

interface Something that allows you to interact with a computer application, such as a database.

Internet A global network of interconnected computers.

logical Something that follows a reasoned and structured pattern, such as the alphabet (A to Z).

MP3 player A device, such as an iPod, that can be used to play digital music files.

online Anything on the Internet.

operational databases Databases that can be changed and updated by users—social networks are built around operational databases.

relational databases Databases that link data together, making it easier to search and browse.

social network A website built around a database (such as Facebook), where users can interact with other users around the world, quickly and easily.

SQL Acronym for Structured Query Language, a computer language used for searching databases.

uploaded Put computer files onto the Internet.

Books

Latta, Sara L. *Cybercrime: Data Trails DO Tell Tales*. Berkeley Heights, NJ: Enslow, 2012.

Lenburg, Jeff. *The Facts on File Guide to Research*. New York, NY: Checkmark Books, 2010.

McGuire, Erin K. *Careers in Database Design* (Careers in Computer Technology). New York, NY: Rosen Publishing Group, 2011.

Oppel, Andy. *Databases DeMYSTiFieD*. New York, NY: McGraw-Hill Osborne Media, 2010.

Roza, Greg. *Databases: Organizing Information* (Digital and Information Literacy). New York, NY: Rosen Publishing Group, 2010.

Websites

Due to the changing nature of Internet links, Rosen Publishing has developed an online list of websites related to the subject of this book. This site is updated regularly. Please use this link to access the list:

http://www.rosenlinks.com/ptech/data